Heaven
without
Hell

HEAVEN WITHOUT HELL

Copyright © 2008

All Rights Reserved.

First Printing 2008

ISBN - 978-0-9747930-1-6

Written by

Brain Miracle

And

Littlest Angel Girl

Dedicated to

Littlest Angel Boy

God is
The source of
infinite
Love and
Understanding

So Heaven was
A Perfectly
happy place
for everyone

Except
For
The Devil

He was not
happy

So
He picked a
fight with his
all-powerful
creator

Was
that
smart?

NO

It was dumb

Does it make sense for him to reject God-the only source of infinite love and understanding

It makes no sense
WHATSOEVER

Can he ever
hope to beat
God in a fight?

Nobody can!

So either he did not *understand* that fighting God is a bad idea...

In which case
he's dumb

Or he couldn't
control
himself...

In which case
he's crazy

So he's dumb
or
crazy

But God would
not *make* him
crazy

It would be
crazy to *make*
him crazy
and...

Then
Send him to
HELL for
being crazy

Because that's
crazy and God
is not crazy

So he's dumb

But is anyone
dumber?

People who sell
their souls to
a dummy

...are pretty dumb

Why?

Because they
fall
for a dumb
trick

They trade
heaven for hell

Is
That
Smart?

No

It's dumb

So Did God Create Hell?

ABSOLUTELY NOT!

Why?

Because a God
of Infinite
Love and
Understanding

Would not
make his
creatures
Dumb!

And then...
Send them to
Hell for being
DUMB!

Because that's
DUMB
And...

God is NOT DUMB

www.ingramcontent.com/pod-product-compliance
Lightning Source LLC
Chambersburg PA
CBHW071840290426
44109CB00017B/1875